ABANDONED!
Towns Without People

BODIE
The Town That Belongs to Ghosts

by Kevin Blake

Consultant: Brad Sturdivant
President, Bodie Foundation
Bridgeport, California

BEARPORT
PUBLISHING

New York, New York

Credits:
Cover and Title Page, © Janelle Lugge/Shutterstock and © Steven Castro/Shutterstock; 4, William Thompson/Heritage Auction Gallery; 4–5, © Paula Cobleigh/Shutterstock; 6, © North Wind Picture Archives/Alamy; 7TL, © claffra/Shutterstock; 7B, © Steven Castro/Shutterstock; 9, © North Wind Picture Archives/Alamy; 10, © SuperStock/Alamy; 11, © Gary Crabbe/Enlightened Images/Alamy; 12, © North Wind Picture Archives/Alamy; 13, Thomas.fanghaenel/Wikimedia; 14, © Doug Meek/Shutterstock; 15, © Hanze/Shutterstock; 16, Daniel Mayer/Wikimedia; 17, © Labusova Olga/Shutterstock; 18–19, © Russ Bishop/Alamy; 19, © worac_sp/Shutterstock; 20, © Gary Saxe/Shutterstock; 21, © Andrea Visconti/Shutterstock; 22, © Laurin Rinder/Shutterstock; 23, Daniel Mayer/Wikimedia; 24, © Arny Raedts/Alamy; 25, Daniel Mayer/Wikimedia; 26, © Xavier Pironet/Shutterstock; 27, © Adam Ziaja/Shutterstock; 28T, William Thompson/Heritage Auction Gallery; 28B, © meunierd/Shutterstock; 29T, © MarcelClemens/Shutterstock; 29B, Daniel Mayer/Wikimedia.

Publisher: Kenn Goin
Senior Editor: Joyce Tavolacci
Creative Director: Spencer Brinker
Design: The Design Lab
Photo Researcher: Jennifer Zeiger

Library of Congress Cataloging-in-Publication Data

Blake, Kevin, 1978–
    Bodie : the town that belongs to ghosts / by Kevin Blake; consultant, Brad Sturdivant, President, Bodie Foundation, Bridgeport, California.
        pages cm. — (Abandoned! Towns without people)
    Includes bibliographical references and index.
    Audience: Ages 7–11.
    ISBN 978-1-62724-524-1 (library binding)—ISBN 1-62724-524-3 (library binding)
    1. Bodie (Calif.)—History—Juvenile literature. 2. Frontier and pioneer life—California—Bodie—Juvenile literature. 3. Ghost towns—California—Juvenile literature. I. Sturdivant, Brad, consultant. II. Title.
    F869.B65B43 2015
    979.4'48—dc23

                              2014029072

For more information, write to Bearport Publishing Company, Inc., 45 West 21st Street, Suite 3B, New York, New York 10010. Printed in the United States of America.

10 9 8 7 6 5 4 3 2 1

Contents

The Town That Vanished

On July 4th, 1880, Bodie, California, was a lively, noisy place. **Citizens** of the town crowded onto Main Street to celebrate the holiday. Among them were **prospectors**, miners, gamblers, and even gunfighters. They were from many different places—from Chicago to China—but they all had something in common. They had come to this dusty, **remote** spot in the mountains to find gold.

Bodie, around 1890

Bodie wouldn't stay crowded for long, however. Within fifty years, the town's Main Street would be filled with a ghostly silence. Today, only five percent of the original buildings are left, and they are slowly crumbling back into the earth. An **eerie** wind blows through their cracked windows. Where did everyone go? What happened to the once-**thriving** town?

Bodie today

In 1880, Bodie and Los Angeles had nearly the same number of people. Today, almost four million people live in Los Angeles—and only a few people live in Bodie.

Eureka!

For most of the 1800s, there was no town of Bodie—only empty, rocky land. In 1848, however, something happened that would change life in many parts of California. Gold was discovered. As a result, more than 300,000 people arrived in the area in a flood of activity that became known as the California Gold Rush. One of them was W. S. Bodey, a businessman from New York.

A man searches for gold in a river during the California Gold Rush.

In the summer of 1859, Bodey and his four partners hiked over California's Sierra Nevada mountains to look for gold. They searched through the rocks and gravel until . . . **eureka**! Bodey found a few glittering **nuggets**. The men had discovered their **fortune**—or so they thought.

The Sierra Nevada mountains

Gold nugget

The Sierra Nevada is a mountain range that stretches between California and Nevada.

Cave-in

Unfortunately, luck ran out for Bodey and his partners after they found gold. That winter, a terrible snowstorm hit the mountains and Bodey froze to death. Not long after, one of Bodey's partners was killed during a fight with a group of Native Americans. The remaining men dug a **mine** and set up a small camp. They dug and dug, searching for more gold. Yet they found little treasure. Bodey's partners soon gave up and left the area. Others took their place, but they also had no luck finding gold.

According to one story, the mining camp was named "Bodie" after a sign painter misspelled Bodey's name.

Bodie is located near the Nevada border.

In 1876, the few people remaining in Bodie were ready to leave. That's when a **cave-in** in the mine shook the camp. The prospectors climbed underground to take a look, certain to find disaster. Instead, they found something wonderful. The walls of the mine were covered in sparkling yellow gold!

To find gold, miners had to dig long, narrow holes, called shafts, with little light to guide them. Sometimes the shafts collapsed, crushing the miners.

Boomtown

News of the gold discovery in Bodie spread quickly. Wagons filled with prospectors from all over the United States arrived daily. **Immigrants** from China boarded ships to California, hoping to find riches to send to their families back home. By 1880, a town that had only 50 people a few years earlier had exploded to a **population** of nearly 10,000!

Prospectors often arrived in Bodie in covered wagons.

As all these new people arrived in Bodie, new businesses popped up. One kind of business did particularly well: **saloons**. There were more than 65 around town. Miners and prospectors gathered in them to listen to music, gamble, and drink alcohol—often getting into trouble as they did so.

A Bodie saloon, once an important gathering place, sits empty today.

In 1880 alone, over $3 million worth of gold was shipped out of Bodie. That's about $50 million in today's dollars.

Wildest Town in the West

Bodie's roughest men hung around in saloons all day and night. Often, they would look for fights to prove their strength. **Brawls** didn't just happen in the town's saloons, however. Lawyers were known to punch their **opponents** in court. Bodie's only doctor even got into a fistfight!

Many of Bodie's fights started in saloons.

More than 90 percent of Bodie's population was male. That's because most of the people who worked in the mines were men.

Yet there were weapons far more dangerous than fists in Bodie. Nearly every man in town carried a **pistol**—and was ready to use it. Shots rang out almost nightly on Main Street, and shootouts were a common way to settle arguments. On many mornings, the church bells didn't ring out the time of day the way other church bells did. Instead, they would ring out the ages of those who had died.

One of Bodie's two churches

Baddest Man in Bodie

Because of all the fights and shootouts, Bodie earned the **reputation** of being home to some very bad men. Mike McGowan might have been the worst. He was known as Man Eater. Why? He liked to bite the noses and ears of the people he fought. While living in Bodie, he had been in so many fights his head was dented!

Anyone who got into a fight with Man Eater or another bad man from Bodie could wind up in a coffin from the town's coffin maker.

In Bodie, Man Eater's terrifying behavior included chomping down on the sheriff's leg, chasing a man down Main Street with a butcher knife, and threatening to bite a policeman's ears off. He once even ate a stray bulldog! Eventually, the police gave him a choice: go to jail or leave town. Man Eater chose to move on.

Dangerous men once prowled these now-empty streets.

In Bodie, the punishment for fighting was $25 or 25 days in jail. Cursing was considered worse. One man caught using bad language was put in prison for 30 days!

The Bodie 601

Even after Man Eater left town, crime was so bad in Bodie that ordinary townspeople decided to take matters into their own hands. They formed the Bodie 601, a **vigilante** group that punished criminals without the help of the police. For example, in 1881, Joseph DeRoche shot and killed Thomas Treloar in the middle of Main Street. When Joseph later broke out of prison, the 601 sprang into action.

The Bodie Jail, over a hundred years after Joseph DeRoche escaped

The 601 hunted down Joseph and, this time, wouldn't allow him the chance to escape. They dragged him to the spot where he had shot Thomas and hanged the murderer from a makeshift **gallows**. While Joseph swung from a rope, a note was pinned to his chest: "All others take warning. Let no one cut him down. Bodie 601."

The 601 tied a rope around Joseph's neck and hanged him.

Although no one is certain, some people say that each number in 601 had a special meaning. *Six* stood for "six feet under"—the depth at which bodies are buried. *Zero* stood for "no trial." *One* stood for "one rope."

The Town Cemetery

After the body of Joseph DeRoche was eventually cut down, it was taken to Bodie's growing cemetery. Yet even the cemetery wasn't always a safe place for a **corpse**. In the middle of the night, grave robbers picked over the bones of the dead for jewelry or other **valuables**. Sometimes, even the body itself was taken.

The Bodie cemetery

One time, after a young woman died of a mysterious illness, curious family members tried to dig up her body to perform an **autopsy**. They were eager to learn what had killed her. Someone, however, didn't want them to solve the mystery. When the family opened her coffin, the woman was gone!

Grave robbers would often leave skulls and other bones scattered around the cemetery.

The Bodie cemetery had a separate section where criminals, such as Joseph DeRoche, were buried.

Going Bust

For many, the chance of striking it rich made up for the danger of living in Bodie. However, by 1882, there was little gold to be found. Out of 30 mines, only two would continue to make money for their owners. New gold mines and **boomtowns** in Arizona and Nevada drew people away from Bodie. As a result, businesses in town had fewer customers and were forced to close.

A row of empty buildings on Main Street in Bodie

As quickly as Bodie had boomed, it went **bust**. By 1884, there were only 1,500 people living there. For every building still occupied in town, three were **abandoned**. Bodie was quickly becoming a **ghost town**.

A kitchen in an abandoned home

People living in Bodie sometimes left their homes in the middle of the night. They would often leave many of their belongings behind.

A Town Destroyed by Jell-O

Bodie had survived gunfights and brawls, booms and busts, but it could not survive a young child upset by his dessert. In the summer of 1932, a teacher served green Jell-O at an end-of-school party. Three-year-old Billy Godward had expected ice cream. The child angrily marched off toward town, found some matches, and lit one near the abandoned Sawdust Saloon.

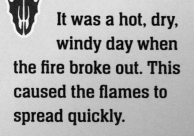

It was a hot, dry, windy day when the fire broke out. This caused the flames to spread quickly.

An abandoned saloon in Bodie

The saloon soon caught fire. Wind blew the flames to other buildings. When the fire department tried to turn on the old fire hoses, only dust and pebbles spurted out. Within an hour, more than 75 percent of the town was destroyed.

The fire destroyed this bank, leaving only its vault intact.

The Curse

With much of Bodie destroyed and few people remaining, thieves came to town to steal whatever items were left behind. They soon realized, however, that they might have taken more than objects with them. Some of them believed they were cursed with terrible luck after stealing from Bodie.

Shelves full of items at the Boone Store

To remove the "curse of Bodie," people would mail stolen items back to the town. Some even sent back rocks that had gotten stuck to their shoes! One family went so far as to write this letter:

> *Dear Bodie:*
>
> *On a recent visit this summer, we found this door knocker in the fields north of your town. Ever since we took it, we've had bad luck, so we would like to return it to its home. . . . Sorry for breaking the rules. I guess we learned our lesson.*
>
> *Sincerely,*
>
> *X the Guilty Party*

Others believe that there is far more than a curse in Bodie. Some visitors have reported that the town is haunted. One story tells about the ghost of a housemaid who was known to attack people in their sleep by sitting on their chests.

Some visitors have reported seeing the ghost of a housemaid living in this house.

The Future of Bodie

Today, only a few people—all park rangers—live in Bodie. The once-noisy saloons are empty, and Main Street has seen its last gunfight. Bodie is just a ghost town with more than 200 buildings slowly crumbling in the hot California sun.

The state of California has tried to keep Bodie in its original state for visitors interested in ghost towns of the Old West.

In 1962, the state of California bought the town of Bodie and opened it as a park for visitors.

Some people, however, think the Bodie gold rush is not quite over. One mining company **estimated** that there may still be billions of dollars of gold in Bodie. One day, there may be a new rush of people coming to the ghost town hoping to find their fortune in gold.

During its boom, Bodie's mines produced over $34 million of gold—or roughly $800 million in today's dollars. Could billions of dollars of gold still remain in Bodie?

Bodie: Then and Now

THEN: An estimated 10,000 people lived in Bodie in 1880.

NOW: Nobody lives in Bodie except for park rangers.

THEN: People traveled around Bodie on horseback or by horse and carriage.

NOW: People travel around Bodie in cars. In the winter, when roadways are blocked with snow, they use snowmobiles.

THEN: In the late 1800s, there were more than 1,600 buildings in Bodie.

NOW: Only about 200 buildings in Bodie are still standing.

THEN: An ounce of gold was worth roughly $20.

NOW: In 2014, an ounce of gold was worth roughly $1,300.

THEN: Bodie was one of the most dangerous places in California, with up to a dozen pistol shots heard every night on Main Street.

NOW: Over 200,000 tourists peacefully visit Bodie State Historic Park every year.

GLOSSARY

abandoned (uh-BAN-duhnd) empty, no longer used

autopsy (AW-top-see) an examination of a dead person to find out the cause of death

boomtowns (BOOM-towns) towns that have grown very rapidly due to successful businesses

brawls (BRAWLS) noisy, rough fights

bust (BUHST) at a point or in a period of having no money

cave-in (KAYV-in) the collapse of a mine or tunnel

citizens (SIT-i-zuhnz) people who live in a particular country, city, or town

corpse (KORPSS) a dead body

eerie (IHR-ee) mysterious, strange

estimated (ESS-ti-*mayt*-id) figured out the approximate amount of something

eureka (yoo-REE-kuh) an excited yell when a discovery has been made

fortune (FOR-chuhn) a very large amount of money

gallows (GAL-ohz) a wooden frame used to hang criminals

ghost town (GOHST TOWN) an empty town with few or no people living there

immigrants (IM-uh-gruhnts) people who come from one country to live in a new one

mine (MINE) a pit or hole where minerals such as gold or silver are dug up from underground

nuggets (NUHG-itz) solid lumps of valuable minerals such as gold

opponents (uh-POH-nuhnts) people who take opposite sides in a fight

pistol (PISS-tuhl) a small gun

population (pop-yuh-LAY-shuhn) the number of people living in a place

prospectors (PROS-pek-turz) people who search the ground for gold, gems, or other valuable resources

remote (ri-MOHT) far away or difficult to reach

reputation (rep-yuh-TAY-shuhn) the opinion that most people have about a person or a place

saloons (suh-LOONZ) places where people buy and drink alcohol

thriving (THRIVE-ing) doing well or growing

valuables (VAL-yoo-uh-buhls) things that are worth a lot of money

vigilante (vij-uh-LAN-tee) a person who is not a police officer who tries to catch and punish criminals

BIBLIOGRAPHY

McGrath, Roger. *Gunfighters, Highwaymen, & Vigilantes: Violence on the Frontier*. Berkeley, CA: University of California Press (1984).

Sprague, Marguerite. *Bodie's Gold: Tall Tales and True History from a California Mining Town*. Reno, NV: University of Nevada Press (2003).

Watson, James, and Doug Brodie. *Big Bad Bodie: High Sierra Ghost Town*. San Francisco: Robert D. Reed (2002).

READ MORE

Friedman, Mel. *The California Gold Rush (True Books)*. New York: Scholastic (2010).

Holub, Joan. *What Was the Gold Rush?* New York: Grosset & Dunlap (2013).

Parvis, Sarah. *Ghost Towns (Scary Places)*. New York: Bearport (2008).

LEARN MORE ONLINE

To learn more about Bodie, visit
www.bearportpublishing.com/Abandoned!

INDEX

ABOUT THE AUTHOR

Kevin Blake lives in Portland, Oregon—not a ghost town!—with his wife, Melissa, and son, Sam. This is his third book for children.